£1.50
12

A SONG OF SI

and other

incorporating
'Week-end in the Village and other verse'

written and illustrated

by

JOHN NURSEY

All proceeds from the sale of this book will be
distributed to selected local charities

OTHER BOOKS BY JOHN NURSEY

'WEEK-END IN THE VILLAGE and other verse'

'RIGHT TO ROAM and other verse'

'SILENT MUSIC and other verse'

'TIME REMEMBERED' (edited)

Published by J.R.Nursey, Forge Cottage, Flaxton, York, YO60 7RW.

Printed and bound by York Publishing Services Ltd.
64 Hallfield Road, Layerthorpe, York, YO31 7ZQ

ISBN 0 9535193 4 1

The cover photograph is of a marshland scene at Beccles in Suffolk.

CONTENTS

A SONG OF SEPTEMBER

A Song of September   7
A Visitor to the Ward   9
To K.I.M.G.   11
A Late Night Encounter   12
A Tour of the House   13
New Year's Eve   15
At Wimbourne Minster   17
An August Reverie   19
The Chiming Clock   21
The Parson's Dilemma   23
The Homecoming   24
The Dress   26
Mortality   28
The Highways Man   29
Exit Stage Right   31
Saturday Afternoon   33
The River   34
Shine, Jesus Shine   37
To Her   39
Those Who Died   40
The Potatoes   44
The Common   45
The Two Heads   47

WEEK-END IN THE VILLAGE

The Wildlife Protectors   48
The Castle Rose Garden   49
The Lead Miners   52
The Soldier's Last Farewell   54
The Local Government Man   55

A River Idyll   57
The Wing Threequarter   60
The Return Visit   62
The Visitor   63
The Prodigal   66
Week-end in the Village   68
Lovely the Wye   71
The Gardener   72
The Apple Blossom   74
The Church's New Foundation   76
At Christmas   79
Justice   80
The Meeting   82
True Love   83

PREFACE

Following the continuing success of its three predecessors this fourth small selection of verse is offered in the hope that it will similarly prove of interest and will enable a generous donation to be made to charitable causes from the proceeds of its sales. 'Week-end in the Village and other verse', the first of the earlier three books, is now no longer available but there remains an interest in the book and a continued demand for copies. In order to satisfy this demand the contents of 'Week-end in the Village' have been added to the new collection and are incorporated into the present volume.

As with the earlier books the verse is supplemented by a number of pen and ink sketches. Few of the sketches, I feel bound to say, are directly associated with the poems and they have been included largely in the hope that they will add to the book's general interest. All are of locations which have a personal nostalgia for me and all are of East Anglian or Yorkshire scenes.

None of the verse has been written for any reason other than my own interest and amusement, and I make no apology for any of the subject matter or content contained in it. Nor do I make any apology for the fact that it is all in a form which rhymes and scans – something seldom bothered with nowadays when more or less anything appears to masquerade as poetry. Many of the poems in this book are of a relatively light-hearted nature and these should not, perhaps, be taken too seriously.

Forge Cottage   John Nursey
Flaxton

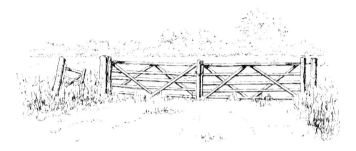

A Song of September

This time of year I love the best
  When early autumn comes,
Victorias, a harvest moon,
  And gold chrysanthemums;

September mists upon the marsh
  Before the sun breaks through
On blackberries along the hedge
  And early morning dew;

The stockyard smell of steaming dung,
  The barn owl's late night call,
And breakfast mushrooms from the field
  Behind the Long Barn wall;

Red berries on the rambling hedge,
  With white-flowered columbine;
Late lingering roses by the wall,
  And elderberry wine.

The roller on the cricket field
  Stands idle till next spring,
And swallows, gathered on the wires,
  Will soon be on the wing.

About the close-cut stubble now
    The scrabbling pheasant struts,
Hard by the wood where we, when boys,
    Would search for hazel nuts.

Ripe apples thick upon the trees
    As days of summer pass,
And longer now the shadows grow
    Across the orchard grass.

The days draw in, the harvest field
    Lies silent now and bare,
The morning grass is wet, and there's
    A nip within the air.

The church is decked with sheaves of corn
    For Harvest Festival,
With turnips, apples, pears, and plums,
    Then supper in the hall.

Now *'All is safely gathered in'*
    We sing in pew and stall,
Regardless whether yields are great
    Or whether yields are small.

Dusk falls by seven; the air is chill,
    The dog fox barks at nights,
And earlier each evening now
    We switch on hearthside lights.

The ever-passing seasons roll
    And winter beckons now;
Across the headland, sure enough,
    Already works the plough.

A Visitor to the Ward

Across the ward from where I lie
The little man sits by his bed,
And in the silence of the room
No patient stirs and nothing's said.

A woman now comes marching in,
Stops at his bed, sits face to face;
Official looking bureaucrat
With trousered suit and business case.

'I am your social worker here,
And things there are I need to know
So we can help when you get home
And sort them out before you go.

What relatives are there at home?
A wife? And is she able to
Give you a hand to get upstairs?
A wheelchair? O dear, that won't do.

Will any neighbours lend a hand?
A sister? Good. Do you get on?
She is forgetful? Never mind;
A week or two then she'll be gone'.

He is a little, private man
And seldom talks save when friends call,
But in the silent, listening ward
His life is now laid bare to all.

'How many bedrooms have you got?
And is your toilet down or up?
And can your wife cook meals for you?
And is she safe with plates and cup?'

Embarrassment we feel for him,
And though we try to close our ear
Within the silence of the ward
We cannot help but lie and hear.

The loud voice more demands to know
As into finance now it delves.
'We'll need, of course, your pension book
So we can check all this ourselves'.

We learn about his son in Wales;
His daughter with her special needs,
And money that he sends each month
To help her with her rent in Leeds.

The woman rises now and goes.
She's talking just outside the door;
'I've finished all my visits here,
Just one more client on Ward Four'.

O how I'd like to march her back
And cross examine, so that we
Could publicly lay bare *Her* life,
And strip her of *Her* dignity.

'Tis such a little thing to ask
That bureaucrats should use some tact,
And show respect for those they serve,
And private things in private act.

To K.I.M.G.

We watched you in the little church
Among the chestnuts and the yews
Baptised and offered unto God,
From round about the carved oak pews.

As in the Vicar's arms you lay
We watched your young untroubled face,
While he, within the Norman font
Anointed you with God's good grace.

And while we watched we wondered then,
As water played upon your head,
What thoughts you might have had of it
Or felt God's blessing in its spread.

We wondered what life holds for you
When twenty years or more have gone;
Though most us will never know
For we, by then, will have moved on.

Will God in his great wisdom give
To you, your mother's gentle grace;
Your father's charm? Will those blue eyes
Make young men turn, your path to trace?

What sort of world will we leave you?
What joys, what turmoil, will there be?
May God go with you; help you make
A better job of it than we.

A Late Night Encounter

Fred Bly was tottering home last night
    Along our village street
When in the evening's fading light
    He did the vicar meet.

"Good evening, Frederick. Drunk again!"
    He heard as they passed by,
And straightaway Fred answered then
    "Ah, vicar, so am I."

A Tour of the House

When I go round a stately home
In parties with a guide
I always find I'm quickly bored
And long to flee outside.

'This portrait is the second Earl,
That next to him, his wife;
And by the stairs, the fourth Earl's son,
Who led a gambling life.

'Behind you, Francis Mortimer.
He added the West Wing
In sixteen ten or thereabouts;
Was steward to the King.

'The inlaid serpentine commode
Is seventeen thirteen.
The ceiling is by Virrio.
And note the carved oak screen.

'The chairs are all by Hepplewhite;
And here across the aisle
The marble pilasters are mock
And formed in Doric style.

'The eighteenth century porcelain
Is French and of the best.'
I stifle – if I can – a yawn,
And try to look impressed.

And always on these guided tours
There'll be, as sure as fate,
One loud-mouthed member of the group
You quickly get to hate.

It's mostly an American,
A female, middle aged;
Who, with the guide, in raucous tones
Is constantly engaged.

'Is that Van Gogh or Constable?
How high up is the dome?
Whose dog is in this photograph?
He's just like ours at home.

'The Cotswolds soon we hope to see
— We're going there with friends —
But we are not quite sure if they
Are open at week-ends.

'Who does this house belong to now?'
In every room she starts.
'And will we get to see', she asks,
'The owner's private parts?'

The earls and dukes upon the walls,
All seem to look at me,
And somehow in their sombre stare
I sense a sort of plea.

'Have sympathy and pity us;
We're left here on display,
And have to put up with all this
Near twenty times a day'.

New Year's Eve

New Year's Eve; the hour of twelve;
Long we gazed upon the sky,
Starlit now across the marsh,
Father's mum and dad, and I;
Round us, silent in the night,
Dairy, cowsheds, barns, and sty.

By the farmhouse kitchen door
Silently with hopes entwined
There we watched the new year in
Hoping future cheer to find,
She with stick, arthritic, frail,
He with pipe and nearly blind.

In his mind the child of seven
Saw the bombs and shells of war
And his Dad and Uncle Frank,
Soldiers on some foreign shore;
Wondering what lay ahead,
What the new year held in store.

Thoughts of Dad kept crowding in –
Rowing river jaunts we'd take;
Days in fields with gun and dog;
Meccano models he could make.
Please, oh please, God, keep him safe;
How that small boy's heart did ache.

Two soldier sons the old pair had
When the new year had begun;
Little could we then have guessed
That before the year was done
War would seek its victims out;
Two would be reduced to one.

Now across the Norfolk marsh
Still I see the starlit glow;
Whether life has proved for me
Good or ill, I do not know,
Since that night when we gazed there
Fifty years and more ago.

At *Wimbourne Minster*

Above the meadows of the Stour
The twin towers of the Minster rise,
This early April morning hour,
In to the azure Dorset skies.

From high upon the western tower
The ancient Quarter Jack looks down,
And heartily rings out the hour
Across the little country town.

Within the church the sun's rays pass
Through windows in the east end gable
And cast the colours of the glass
Upon the white clad altar table.

Through Norman nave and choir and tower,
Past tombs of Beauforts, Ettrickes, Bankes,
I chance to come, this early hour,
In to the crypt the chapel flanks.

A copied Raphael on the wall,
Three aisles with pillars ranging through,
A fine rib-vaulted roof, and all
Restored in nineteen twenty two.

Down here within this hallowed place
Descended to by wide stone stair,
A woman sits, with careworn face,
Her eyelids closed in silent prayer.

Advanced in years and frail of limb
Alone among the rows of chairs
She sits, hands clasped, and speaks to Him,
Unburdening her needs and cares.

What silent words are passing there?
I wonder, as she sits and prays;
Of my own presence unaware
Or of my momentary gaze.

Perhaps there is a troubled friend;
Perhaps some feud that brings her grief;
A close relation at life's end;
Perhaps her own time left is brief.

Now life is on its downward slope
And ageing limbs grow weak and numb
Does she, perhaps, now pray of hope
For an eternal life to come?

Among the tombs and figured brass
Where kings and poor alike have trod,
I ponder, as I quietly pass,
And leave her there alone with God.

An August Reverie

I came down from the moor today
To meadow, hedge, and lane, and stile,
And in the scene that round me lay
I idly stood and dreamed awhile.

A drowsy calm of afternoon;
A cloudless sky, and no sound heard;
The rambling hedge with brambles strewn;
And silent fields where nothing stirred.

I thought, while leaning on a fence,
This lovely sight confronting me
When I stand here a twelvemonth hence
Once more as beautiful will be.

Though soon this summer scene will fade
The earth will stir and flower once more;
A thousand summers has it made
And each as lovely as before.

The bindweed in the hedge will show
Once more its trumpets white and gay,
And butterflies flit to and fro
Round meadow-sweet along the way.

The seasons' pattern onward steers;
What difference then a twelvemonth on?
None, save of my remaining years
Another will have come and gone.

The seasons come, the seasons go,
Each showing as it did before;
Unendingly God makes it so;
While man decays and comes no more.

In fifty years, perhaps, will lean
Upon this fence some passer by,
Who'll gaze upon this self-same scene
And love its beauty just as I.

The Chiming Clock

When half awake at night I lie
And hear downstairs the old clock chime
My mind drifts back to boyhood days,
A distant and a happier time.

My uncle's house and Suffolk coast
With cliffs, and gulls, and sandy shore,
And summer air, and picnic teas,
And mem'ries that crowd in once more.

This chiming clock the couple owned
– A present on their wedding day –
Stood fifty years upon their shelf,
Till came the time they passed away.

Yet still I see them clearly now –
She busy sewing by the hearth;
In railway cap and uniform
He coming up the garden path.

He and Fred Hall – the station staff
There at that little seaside place,
Upon the grass-green Suffolk cliffs
Where days of youthful joy I'd trace.

Through cliff-top stations ran the line;
Their names – what magic lay in each!
Through Corton, Hopton, Low'stoft North,
And Gorleston Links to Yarmouth Beach.

Within the chimes I see again
The station clock with homely tick,
A fire ablaze in the office grate
When days were raw and snow lay thick.

I see again the station bridge,
Where often in the War I'd be
To watch the planes fly up and down
At target practice out at sea.

In later years on Christmas nights
To cliff-top camps the cockneys came
From off the trains; their passage lit
By village boys with lamps aflame.

When winter winds raged round about
I see the cottage warm fire's glow;
And on the grass the little house
My uncle built in head-high snow.

The chimes resound, the same as then,
But time itself moves ever on;
New houses now engulf the place,
The little station is long gone.

The railway cottages are all
Now tarted up, with strip pine floors,
And owned by smart executives
With Aga stoves and Four by Fours.

How little of that place they know,
What life, what actions did befall;
While constantly the old clock speaks
To me, of scenes long past recall.

The Parson's Dilemma

Our vicar was appointed here
    From some far distant town
Where he had been accustomed to
    A life of cap and gown.

To get to know our parish flock
    He did himself apply,
And early in his visits called
    On Fred and Gertrude Bly.

He talked of plans for Sunday church
    While he sat drinking tea,
Then said 'I wonder if you'd give
    A bit of help to me.

'As you may know I'm city bred
    And I am in some doubt.
I've never preached to country folk;
    What should I preach about?'

What preach about? He wanted help,
    Some guidance, as it were.
Fred thought a bit and then replied
    'About five minutes, sir.'

The Homecoming

What joy to me when I came home
    To Suffolk lanes once more
And felt the sea-wind in my face
    Along the Dunwich shore.

Back home among the Suffolk men
    I knew when I was young,
With Suffolk mud upon their boots,
    Broad Suffolk on their tongue;

Staunch independence in their eye,
    Dry humour in their jokes,
Good friends and true, and resolute
    As time-worn English oaks.

Back home to fields and open skies
    Where men have time to think,
And live in homely cottages
    Of flint or Suffolk pink.

Old Gilbert with his battered cap
  And drooping black moustache,
Now bringing up the ambling cows
  For milking, from the marsh.

Fred Wilson plodding round the yard
  In old familiar form,
And Alfie's van parked at the gate,
  With bread new-baked and warm.

Once more I'd see the great elms rise
  Against a Suffolk sky,
And know that summer would be good
  If rooks were building high.

Now I could roam old haunts again;
  The cliff-tops at Covehithe,
And ivied towers and marshland mills
  By Waveney, Bure and Blyth.

And at the ancient Wherry Inn
  To where I often strode
Drink Adnams ale and idly talk
  Of news from Carrow Road.

Ah! joy it is to be among
  The men of one's own kind
With London streets and London smoke
  For ever left behind.

The Dress

Down the little winding street
At a dress shop we stopped by,
Where a gown hung trim and neat,
Softly red, and took your eye.

Fine you looked when you appeared
From the Fitting Rooms and screens;
How you loved the dress but feared
Cost was far beyond your means.

Other shopping you pursued,
In your thoughts that dress all day;
Till at last you did conclude
You must buy it come what may.

To the shop we made our way,
There with heartache to be told
'Sad, but we regret to say
Since you called the dress was sold.'

Downcast then, all rapture gone,
Naught for comfort could you draw;
Losing what your heart's set on
Makes you want it all the more.

Sad the journey back from town,
But to find when home again
There a package; there the gown.
O what joy on your face then!

While our separate ways went we
I'd returned and bought the dress;
Got the shop-girl to agree
When we'd call, she'd not confess.

Strange how clear they linger on,
Such fond memories as this,
From those years long distant gone,
Years of joy and youthful bliss.

Often down that street I go;
Gone, the shop; and long gone, you;
Yet that day still haunts me so,
When for us the skies were blue.

Mortality

Of all the gardening jobs I do
The one that I most dread
Is going round with secateurs
The roses to dead-head.
As I lop off each fading flower
And see it lying there,
I always contemplate and think
How well I am aware
That had I not been born a man
And was a rose instead,
By now, someone with secateurs
Would have cut off my head.

The Highways Man

I am a Council highways man, my job's to put up signs,
And dig up roads, do traffic counts, and paint more yellow lines.
In winter months we're seldom seen, but then come out like drones
In summer at Bank Holidays with miles of traffic cones.

So we can speed the traffic up we widen roads; and then
Lay humps across the carriageway to slow it down again.
Our highways work is carefully planned, and what we aim for most
Is August, where the populace is heading for the coast.

It gives a sort of inner glow to see the queues stopped dead
Beyond the temporary sign – *'Roadworks five miles ahead;'*
And what a laugh – those fatuous signs to make it look okay:
'Repairing worn out Carriageway' and *'Sorry for Delay.'*

It adds to all the fun when we can think up something new
To help confuse the motorist and get him in a stew.
'No entry here from ten till four, except on certain days,
When this applies from nine till five and Single Lane displays.'

29

I have no time for motorists, a curse is what they are;
Of all humanity the worst, my sort of own bêtes noires.
Down quiet roads where owners park I make them yell a bit
By putting up *'No Parking'* signs just for the hell of it.

We do our best to urbanise the tranquil village scene
With kerbs, and signs; and widen roads with tarmac in the Green.
We hate to leave the road unmarked – it looks so bland and bare –
So paint on hatching and white lines, and arrows everywhere.

Though obvious to any fool, it's always on the cards
There'll be a sign – *'No footway for the next two hundred yards;'*
And also huge electric signs to add a touch of town,
Which flash at you as you go past and tell you to *'SLOW DOWN.'*

For Traffic Orders I'm your man, I raise them on a whim
To hinder Johnny Motorist and make life hell for him;
The smell of steamy boiling tar, and yellow lines, and white,
And miles and miles of traffic queues, I dream of every night.

Exit Stage Right

My friend's a sort of Acting chap
    Of modest local fame,
Although, 'tis true, the chances are
    You've never heard his name.

Most parts he takes are men who die
    Quite early in the play,
So he can spend Acts Two and Three
    In pubs across the way.

Dramatic are his entrances
    Since they are mostly late,
But once on stage his booming voice
    Makes scenery vibrate.

His sword fights are a fearsome sight,
    Arms flailing in attack.
So if you go to see his plays
    Get seats well to the back.

His public readings of my verse
    Make evenings grim and long;
He ponces all about the stage,
    And gets the wording wrong.

And at his theatre in the town
    The winter seasons pass
With many a Shakespeare tragedy
    Transformed to Whitehall farce.

He's bold and brash and versatile,
    Does Chekhov, Shaw, and Coward;
No-one, like he, can make Macbeth
    Sound just like Frankie Howerd.

When seats don't sell he summons me,
    And sundry other folk;
Which means the audience that night
    Is doubled at a stroke.

We tell him that he's very good,
    That he's done well in life;
(Though there's some truth in this, because
    He's got a lovely wife.)

At heart he is a splendid chap
    Who does his best and tries,
And we are sure he'll get good parts
    In Heaven when he dies.

Saturday Afternoon

Is it you that I hear at the garden gate,
Coming home from the town with your shopping done?
As the Saturday afternoon grows late,
And the teatime news has just begun.

Ah, no; the familiar sound that I catch,
As I yearn for the enterer there to be you,
Is merely the wind as it rattles the latch,
And naught but a memory passes through.

How constantly, still, I am drawn to reflect
On your Saturday trips that are now no more;
And still, as I listen, I half expect
At teatime to hear you return as before.

No more will the latch know the touch of your fingers;
The girl at the gate now lies silent and still.
Of our life at its best just a memory lingers,
And the wind on the latch that haunts me at will.

The River

With rod and line on days of ease
    My path to Waveney leads,
Where nothing stirs except a breeze
    That whispers in the reeds.

The river, silent, clear, and still,
    By alder, ash, and birch
Winds slowly down past Dunburgh Hill,
    Across from Barsham Church.

Two counties of this eastern slab
    Along the Waveney draw;
One gave us Constable and Crabbe,
    The other Nelson bore.

Among the reeds and bankside grass
    I idly sit and dream,
See phantoms of old wherries pass
    Along the languid stream.

Their great sails stirring in the breeze
    As once they might have been,
In silence moving through the trees
    Across the marshland scene.

A warbler in the far bank trees,
　　A songster bright and hale;
Such lovely notes; no wonder he's
　　Called Broadland nightingale.

Among the reeds small dabchicks play;
　　Contented here I feel,
Though nothing do I catch all day
　　Except one trifling eel.

To boyhood days I backward look,
　　See clear on Beccles Quay
With rod and line and bent pin hook
　　Dick, Peter, John, and me.

On summer boating jaunts we four
　　Would spend our hours of play;
Row by the Church and Puddingmoor
　　And head up Gel'ston way.

Towards the lock our way we'd trace
　　Where we would idly float
Close by the Inn – an ancient place,
　　Where beer was brought by boat.

Around its fire, with ale would sit
　　The marshmen of the fen;
This place remote, and oil-lamp lit,
　　With ghosts of wherrymen.

Marsh buttercups the June days bring,
　　With rue and cuckooflower;
While out across the Waveney ring
　　The bells of Beccles tower.

So softly does the river glide
    By meadows, lanes, and mills;
Past Beccles Church and riverside,
    And on to Boater's Hills.

What joy for us that we should miss
    The coachloads by the hour
Had Constable been born at Diss
    And not upon the Stour.

What beauty in this river lies!
    What magic lingers there
From Redgrave birth, to where it dies
    In Breydon and the Yare.

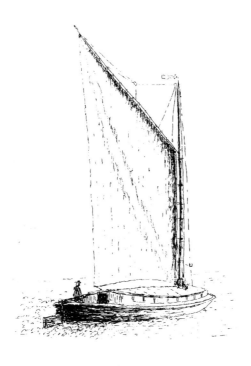

Shine Jesus Shine
(*A hymn of our time*)

Shine Jesus shine
    And please be my best friend,
And please be there to welcome me
    When life is at its end.

God bless us each and every day
    Send down your love divine,
And when I do the Lottery
    Please make the jackpot mine.

Please feed all starving children Lord
    And give them what they need,
And when I trip on Tesco's floor
    Please help my Claim succeed.

Grant single mothers what they ask
    And make the fathers pay;
And if you can give yet more powers
    Unto the C.S.A.

Bless all asylum seekers, Lord
    In countries far and near;
Find them, O Lord, somewhere to live,
    But somewhere not round here

From trendy liberals save us Lord;
    Especially set us free
From writers on *The Guardian*
    And all the BBC.

Lord help me lead a holy life
   Till up in Heaven we meet,
And may things, please, turn out all right
   In Coronation Street.

O help me love my fellow men,
   Please keep me free from sin;
And when the next election comes
   Help Labour to get in.

Don't let me be a NIMBY Lord
   But don't let them allow
New houses on the field next door,
   Please keep it free somehow.

Grant us, O Lord, thy love divine,
   Bring peace to every nation,
And may my next year's pay increase
   Be well above inflation.

Lord grant these favours unto me,
   Make me a happy man;
And if you do you know that I
   Will love you all I can.

To Her

So much in life I would not lose,
But what I could not bear
Would be one day to wake and turn
And find you were not there.

Those Who Died

Around the church the trees stand bare
Against the winter sky,
Below the lonely brooding moor,
With tumbling stream close by.
A haven from the icy chill
That grips the morning dale,
With Ingleborough and Whernside peaks
Enrapt in misty veil.

A little church of stolid build,
No idle pomp or fuss;
A stone flagged floor, a stone clad roof
On heavy timber truss.
The nave and chancel all in one,
Of simple form and line;
Scarce fifty feet, and much rebuilt
In eighteen sixty nine.

A Midland Railway tablet here
In memory of its dead,
Men killed while working on the line
From Settle to Dent Head.
Within the stillness of the church
I browse with idle thought
Through records of the railway years
And of the grief they brought.

Of men who laboured at Blea Moor,
Two miles or so from here;
A savage place, remote, and wild,
And windy, cold, and drear.
In shanty huts the families lived
Within that dismal scene,
At Inkerman, Sebastopol,
Dent Head, and Batty Green.

From brickworks' chimneys smoke and soot
Poured forth in acrid trail,
While blasting from the tunnel works
Re-echoed through the dale.
In mud and bog and boulder clay
Hard was the life men led;
And hard they toiled and hard they drank,
And hard the violence bred.

Men, women, children, – sad the tales
These sombre pages tell;
Two hundred souls lie buried here
From hutments in the Fell.
Huts rat infested, cramped, and foul,
With cesspits by the door;
No sanitation; squalid, and
Diseases by the score.

Of smallpox, cholera, I read,
And accidents to men;
So many deaths, and over half
Were children under ten.
Of blood, I read, crushed bones, and death
From wagons breaking loose,
Carts overturning, navvies killed
Through dynamite misuse.

I join again the Whernside scene,
A land of crags and caves,
Where snowdrops in the winter sun
Show white among the graves.
So peaceful now the churchyard lies;
'Tis hard to think such woe
And sadness did engulf this place
A hundred years ago.

So many graves and grassy mounds
Erected at this place;
Now disappeared, all levelled out
With no surviving trace.
The railway dead a churchyard plaque
Does solemnly recall,
To supplement the tablet stone
Upon the church west wall.

Yet up the dale at Ribblehead
A greater tribute stands –
The proud and massive viaduct
These built with their own hands.
Full square across the Pennine scene
This legacy survives
Of wives and children, and the men
Who toiled and lost their lives.

How few today, on railway jaunts
From Settle to Carlisle,
Would guess the cost in human life
Of every scenic mile;
Or as they pass by Ribblehead
Would ever understand
What hardship was endured by these
Here sleeping close at hand.

The Potatoes

His neighbour leant upon Fred's gate,
  A red-faced man and small;
A clever dick who'd tell you straight,
  And thought he knew it all.

'Your spuds aren't very large,' he said,
  'I wonder what's the cause.'
'Ah well, I grow them,' answered Fred,
  'To fit my mouth, not yours.

The Common

What magic in the winter snow when crisp's the air and chill,
When trees and brushwood all about, stand silent, white, and still.
Spring sunshine filtering through the trees; such beauty stirs the heart.
Far from the rush of life and din this is a world apart.

But now the Common's being cleared, and someone has decreed
These woods and trees aren't wanted now; more heath is what we need.
Green woodpeckers will nest no more down in the corner wood;
The trees, the birds, the leafy paths, will soon be gone for good.

No more the tawny owl at nights will flitter through the trees;
No more the birch will softly sway in summer's gentle breeze.
Ah! lovely graceful silver birch, they've got it in for you.
You'll all be gone, and sold for logs, within a year or two.

At first it was the Wildlife Trust with self-applauding pride,
Who thought we'd slap them on the back for what they would provide.
But when they found that public rage was what prevailed instead
Their profile faded; now the work is English Nature led.

And English Nature put up bills, with screeds of platitudes,
In hope that local people would revise their attitudes.
But local people did not care for bureaucrats from town
With fatuous posters; so the bills were very soon torn down.

No consultation; no-one asked, before the work begun;
This quango and the Wildlife Trust are answerable to none.
They prattle on, of this and that, all wooded commons lack.
'Besides,' they say, 'we think, in time, marsh gentians will come back.'

Important are the trees, they said, upon the lowland scene;
Yet all they leave is, here and there, a token evergreen.
Occasionally they leave a birch to stand against the sky;
But don't be fooled – they're all ring barked, to make them slowly die.

The quiet secluded brookside path is cleared and now lies bare,
And saunterers there are now exposed to gawping motorists' stare.
Old woods are being swept away, and soon will come the day
Across the waste we'll see the cars, on roads a mile away.

Already desolation grows by every path and track,
And little comfort 'tis to know marsh gentians will come back.
Oh, honest, little, friendly flower, of dreamy azure blue,
How can you know, when you return, what price we've paid for you.

The Two Heads

When Cromwell had his head cut off
They put it on display,
And in a room at Charlton House
It sits there to this day.

Appropriate this venue was
For now they have the pair;
In each of two glass cabinets
A withered head sits there.

A grisly sight the two heads make,
Each with its shrivelled face;
But so would yours be if you'd been
Five centuries in a case.

These shrunken skulls – I recommend
You see them if you can;
One's Cromwell's when he was a boy
The other when a man.

The Wildlife Protectors

They fix a notice on the gates,
    Where moorland trackways go.
'Keep clear of nesting birds,' it states,
    'Respect for wildlife, show.'

They come again when Autumn bites;
    Their gundogs standing by,
They line the birds up in their sights
    And blast them from the sky.

The Castle Rose Garden

Why does this garden haunt me so?
   What magic does it hold,
To fill me with such rapturous glow
   While others leave me cold?

Such wealth of fragrance and of hue
   In all the beds around!
With haunting names the garden through
   Of roses that abound.

Old friends from literature are here
   By every grass trimmed path;
The Reeve, The Squire, Ophelia,
   Jude, and the Wife of Bath.

Lucetta, keeping far at bay
   The Mayor of Casterbridge;
A Shropshire Lad, and Rose de L'Hay,
   May Queen, and Heritage.

Soft pink against the old yew hedge
   Grows Empress Josephine;
And straggling at the border's edge
   A rampant Eglantine.

All white on the pergola now
   The Rambling Rector trails;
While Albertine each year somehow
   The arbour oversails.

The lavender is everywhere
   Alive with murmuring bees;
A blackbird calls from somewhere there
   Among the apple trees.

All through the trees white roses sprawl,
   Each clambering from the base;
While on the grass its shadows fall
   Like patterns of old lace.

Late Summer in the morning light
   The pinks in radiance grow,
With Mrs. Sinkins' fragrant white,
   And red of Devon Glow.

Delphiniums, of stately grace
   A month or so ago,
Are all now gone, and in their place
   The agapanthus' show.

Thank God for the creating hands
   That made a heaven like this;
And for the loud Americans
   Who give the place a miss.

The owner brought all this about,
  Restored the place to life;
Designed the beds and laid them out
  In memory of his wife.

I saw him once in here alone,
  In quiet solitude.
A stranger there and unbeknown
  I felt I did intrude.

I felt within me at that hour,
  And somehow thought it right,
For him alone each rose and flower
  Made such a lovely sight.

The garden, with its old brick walls,
  And sundial, rose, and pond,
Stands silent as the evening falls,
  A hallowed mantle donned.

Such joy to me sets this apart,
  Though why, I do not know;
But something strikes within my heart,
  And makes it haunt me so.

The Lead Miners

I climb the lonely hillside path;
    The way is steep and slow;
I pause for breath, and in the Dale
    See Reeth lie far below.

Two hundred years ago and more
    How different this path then;
With steady streams of mining carts,
    And trudging mining men.

In winter's dark they climbed the hill
    Before the morning light;
Went underground; and then emerged
    To see the black of night.

Five hundred feet below the ground
    The lead mine had its hub;
Along the Levels miners toiled,
    With pick and rail and tub.

By candlelight they spent their days,
    In space enough to squeeze
Through tunnels long and dark and damp;
    With worsening lung disease.

On many great cathedrals now
    The lead which does survive
Was won by these who rasped and coughed,
    And died at forty five.

They led a hard but homely life
    By hearth at eventide;
Their houses now are week-end homes,
    With four-wheel drives outside.

In brass bands at the Institute,
    Where practice nights were held,
They played at Muker, Reeth, and Thwaite,
    At Gunnerside, and Keld.

But economics closed the mines
    By eighteen eighty eight;
The mining men then had no choice
    But up and emigrate.

I rest close by a tall brick stack,
    Now silent, cold, and still;
Then see the sun break through the cloud,
    And shine on Calver Hill.

Across the moor from where I gaze,
    The grass-grown trackway cuts
To where the waste heaps from the mine
    Now mix with Shooting Butts.

A mining hamlet lies close by,
    But time has done its worst;
Three houses and some crumbling barns
    Are all that's left of Hurst.

The air is crisp and brightly clear,
    A plover calls nearby;
And gently rustles in the breeze
    The heather where I lie.

I count life's blessings that are mine,
    That these men never got;
And feel a great humility,
    At this lonely moorland spot.

The Soldier's Last Farewell

Alone we stood by the cottage door,
In the glow from the Kitchen light,
My father and I, on the winter's night
When he went away to the War.

I knew that this was his last farewell
Before sailing to foreign shores;
And though it was all in a noble cause
I'd a sadness I could not quell.

Though only seven I knew the score,
And what dangers lay waiting ahead
From shellfire and bombs; and to what it led
When you fought in a bloody war.

'Look after your mother, my boy,' he said,
Though at seven I scarcely guessed
How apt were his words as my hand he pressed,
And some tears I began to shed.

He held me close in the pallid light,
Then turned, and I followed the sound
Of the tread of his boots on the frosty ground
As they faded into the night.

The Local Government Man

I came as just a junior clerk.
    A month or two I spent,
And then I got in with the Chief
    And up the ladder went.

A managerial post I got,
    It suited more my style.
I grew a beard, and wrote reports
    Advancing my profile.

I am proactive, broadly based,
    Not too much overkill.
I wrapped them all in knots with my
    Communications skill.

I'm well in with the Leader now,
    So when my Chief was sacked
They elevated me a bit.
    A lot, in point of fact.

I am a hands-on leader now.
    My job's to interface
With multi-cultural council staff,
    And watch the database.

Autonomous and integral,
    There's so much to address;
With feedback to the councillors,
    Their business to progress.

I'm working on a Corporate Plan,
    Which suits my focussed taste.
With in-put from consulted groups
    To make it client based.

I've got a good track record now.
    I'm busy heading up
The challenging scenario
    That lies within my cup.

You don't know what I'm on about?
    Well, really nor do I.
We have to use this language now;
    It's how we all get by.

Besides, when Council meetings come,
    No matter what I say,
I know that if I talk like this
    I'll always get my way.

Your average councillor these days
    Is not so very bright.
He sits in meetings in his jeans;
    Thinks what I want is right.

Excuse me, but I must press on.
    Reports to activate,
A strategy to put in place,
    And staff co-ordinate.

A River Idyll

The dipping oars the only sound
As my boat glides on with easy run,
And the bankside willows all around
Sway softly in the Suffolk sun.

My thoughts go back to such a day,
To a boyhood scene, enacted when
My father rowed us up this way,
And life to me was joyful then.

The two of us – just man and son,
Just a trip in a boat, yet how set
Was the memory when the day was done,
That I would never quite forget.

A kingfisher all brightly blue,
I remember, on a fallen tree;
And with such grace and brilliant hue
It seemed a lovely thing to me.

We edged the boat in to the side,
Where a half sunk rotting houseboat lay;
And then the bird with a sudden glide
Across the river flew away.

Alone I sat on the sunken wreck
As I watched with pride my father dive
With agile ease from the houseboat deck,
And then strike out with powerful drive.

I sensed the ease and natural grace
Of the athlete, as I watched him swim
With majestic glide and flashing pace.
Oh, how I hoped I'd be like him.

He dressed, cast off, and then we slid
Out from the wreck and that bankside spot.
How far we went and what else we did
I do not know and it matters not.

When we got home he promised me
We'd go again when his leave came round;
Take out the boat on another spree,
And for the houseboat we'd be bound.

But when next Summer came around
In a far-off blazing desert sun
He lay stark still below the ground;
His river outings were all done.

The swaying willows seem to say,
As I paddle by in wistful thought,
'So fine a life to be snatched away,
While yours went on and came to naught.'

And yet that scene, which does not dim,
Implanted in the child of seven,
Of the bird and boat and his father's swim,
Remains for me a glimpse of Heaven.

The Wing Threequarter

Fast down the wing I used to run,
    The ball beneath my arm;
Opponents trailing in my wake,
    Spreadeagled by my palm.

Sometimes they'd cry 'Well played old chap,'
    The team-mates at my side;
The lads who thirty years ago
    Could match me stride for stride.

Now we are all in middle age,
    On separate paths long set.
Long gone the greetings warm and keen
    On match days when we met.

All life seemed then a rugby match;
    Of little else we'd speak
But of the game next Saturday;
    We lived from week to week.

The Dressing Room is still the same,
    With smell of Wintergreen,
Hot steaming water in the bath,
    And smeared-on vaseline.

The winger worries now as then
    About the way he'll play;
About the wing opposing him,
    A County man, they say.

'Will he run round me as he sprints;
    Evade my outstretched dive,
And make me look a useless fool
    No matter how I strive?'

'And will I drop the crucial pass
    When open gaps appear?
Or will I score a try that makes
    The crowd stand up and cheer?'

Late Summer on the new mown pitch
    At nights we used to train.
We'd stretch our unconditioned limbs;
    The blood would stir again.

Our hopes were high for the season,
    And the games that lay ahead;
For fixtures that we had to win,
    And those we viewed with dread.

Though I am fifty years and more
    The blood it rises still;
But gone's the young athletic man,
    Whose swerve could raise a thrill.

Oh, why is it our hearts still yearn
    For things old bones do not?
For the speed of limb and muscle,
    The young alone have got.

I stand and watch from the touchline
    My son sprint by to score,
With blistering pace down the wing where
    His father went before.

I know that there is part of me
    Still out there in the game,
And as he races home to score
    The joy is still the same.

The Return Visit

We lay and talked all through the night
Till dawn began to show;
We saw then, in the morning light,
The Dale all white with snow.
The homely Inn; the winter scene;
The joy that we did share;
I wondered if there'd ever been
A happier loving pair.

Again the Inn; again that sight;
Though youth and years have flown.
Again I've had a sleepless night;
But this time on my own.
Long gone the girl whose love I had,
And empty is my heart.
I wonder if the roads are bad,
And if my car will start.

The Visitor

Along the gravel path I toil,
    On an autumn day set bright and fair.
With joy I tread our native soil,
    And breathe again the Norfolk air.

I call upon you when I can
    And I know these days you never roam;
For since my visits first began
    I always find you here at home.

I think of some odd distant day
    And recall our happy carefree hours,
Each time I climb this winding way,
    With my feeble bunch of new-bought flowers.

I sometimes think of Marshland Lane,
   Where we lingered in the evening sun,
The day I met you off the train
   From College, when your term was done.

Do you still ponder now and then
   On scenes portrayed in our wedding book?
And how we always smiled again
   At photographs old Naylor took?

My uncle in his farming boots;
   And your great-aunt with her bearlike hugs;
And Bill and I in our morning suits,
   A pair of gruesome rugby thugs.

Do you recall the Brecon Hills?
   And the way we had to deviate
To find hotels with lower bills,
   When touring in my Morris Eight?

And how the old car proved no wreck,
   Though the hills got higher and higher?
And uncle Albert's wedding cheque
   We had to spend on a tyre?

Fine upright men our boys have grown;
   To be sure you would be proud and glad.
One's got the daughters of his own
   We yearned, but somehow never had.

I read the words carved on your stone;
   Can there really be so much time gone,
Since you departed on your own
   And left me here to struggle on?

I often dream how shadows play
    On your name set here upon this heath,
And sometimes long for the coming day
    When mine is added underneath.

I fill the vase, arrange the flowers,
    With heavy heart and moistened eye;
Then leave you to your silent hours,
    With friends all sleeping quietly by.

The Prodigal

I never really liked him much,
    As far as I recall.
He seemed to have no common touch,
    And thought he knew it all.

I cannot say I knew him well,
    Not often our paths crossed;
But when they did we did not dwell,
    And little love was lost.

Eventually he left the scene,
    Retired from college life;
The academic, who had been
    Sharp tongued, a man of strife.

In later years I found he had
    Returned to his home town;
The place where he had been a lad,
    And there he'd settled down.

Once back in his own town, it seems,
    He'd shown a different face;
Now he could realise his dreams
    Of working for the place.

He published books of photographs
    Collected of the town,
With notes and detailed paragraphs
    All lovingly set down.

The Preservation Trust he chaired
    With enterprising sway;
Saved many buildings, which were spared
    From crumbling in decay.

He smartened up each little wynd
    That wound around the town,
Neglected, and not often signed,
    And generally run down.

Near both the Green and Castle side
    His house lay neat and trim.
They put a plaque up when he died:
    '*These meant so much to him.*'

For all he did the town was glad
    That he'd come home at last.
And then I wondered if I had
    Misjudged him in the past.

Perhaps he'd hated teaching days,
    And students got him down;
Incited his short tempered ways,
    And thought he was a clown.

Perhaps that man who'd loved this place,
    Such earlier cares had borne;
And truly was of quiet grace,
    Unworthy of my scorn.

I know that when I pass that plaque
    And look up at his name,
I sense him somehow looking back,
    And turn my head in shame.

Week-end in the Village

There's a party at the Rectory,
  Though it's not a rectory now.
No sleep for us till two or three.
  Till then, a constant row.

It's Thump, Thump, Thump, from the music;
  The beat's what drives you mad.
Thank God it's Sunday when we'll wake;
  For that at least, we're glad.

We wake next day to cheerful song
  Of blackbird, wren, and tit.
Then starts a strimmer's raucous whine
  From Swale House, opposite.

Mid morning sees the mowers out,
  And people with their dogs.
At Willy Peel's a chain saw rasps,
  At work on next year's logs.

The Swale House owner's working hard
  A new porch to append;
Which by degrees, with hammering,
  Progresses each week-end.

He is restricted in his work,
  An office man all week.
So Sunday is the time for him,
  His workday, so to speak.

On Saturdays it's fairly quiet,
  At least till evening comes;
Unless you count the yapping din
  Of poodles at the Lumbs'.

We've all got dogs that bark and howl,
    And sometimes two or more.
The average now along our row
    Is nearly one point four.

A sort of builder occupied
    The house next door to me.
He and his mates at each week-end
    Worked with a constancy.

They banged and drilled from morn to night,
    They hardly paused at all;
And most of it, it seemed to me,
    Was on my Front Room wall.

Then when they'd done he moved away.
    But, Oh dear! What a curse.
A DIY man bought the house,
    And he was even worse.

With windows out, and new doors in,
    He hammered with a will.
'For six days shalt thou toil and bang,
    The seventh, louder still.'

For week-end jobs he is your man,
    A housing problem fixer;
With drill, and saw, and bright ideas
    That need a concrete mixer.

One week no noise – so out we go
    To lounge the evening through;
Then strongly comes the pungent smell
    Of someone's barbecue.

On Sundays after tea, at six
　We hear the school clock strike.
Then from next door there comes a sound
　Like a revving motor bike.

It's a sit-on motor mower;
　And Sunday evenings pass,
My neighbour driving up and down,
　To cut his orchard grass.

Hurrah! The DIY man's gone.
　His work next door is through.
He's busy with his bag of tools
　And fixing somewhere new.

A nice young man's come in his place.
　He has to bang at nights
To rectify the DIY
　And put the place to rights.

I go outside to lock the sheds,
　It's getting on for ten;
There's Thump, Thump, Thump, from the Harveys';
　There's a party at The Glen.

Lovely the Wye

Lovely the Wye in the summer sun;
 And the Teme by Ludlow tower,
Where the cuckoo calls, and the old church clock
 Plays hymn tunes on the hour.

Lovely the sound of the curlew's call
 In the wild green Arran hills;
And the morning sun over Brodick Bay
 My heart with pleasure fills.

Lovely the sweep of a Suffolk sky
 Over marsh and meadow green;
When the sun goes down and the wild geese fly,
 In the twilight barely seen.

Lovely all these, and the memory's sweet,
 As the moonlight on the sea.
But dearer by far is the one I love,
 Who means so much to me.

The Gardener

Eighty years and a walking frame,
Old Jill moves through the beds,
To where he forks round the Esther Reads,
With their soft white daisy heads.

'There are buds on the Danse de Feu,' she said,
'I think it'll be all right.
And the pruning you did to the Albertine
Has given the Phlox more light.'

Her face lights up with an ancient smile;
The garden had been her joy.
'I'm ever so pleased with what you've done.'
Like a child with a new found toy.

His house at home seemed cheerless,
Long lost to woman's touch;
With sour unfriendly neighbours,
Who did not like him much.

He wondered what life's future held;
What purpose was there left.
But the grateful smile and the kindly word –
All hope was not bereft.

'Tis queer how life's contentment
Can be found in curious ways;
By giving unsuspected joy
With simple gardening days.

The Apple Blossom

The apple in the Orchard
Is hung with blossom round,
And celandines unnumbered
Grow thick upon the ground.

And all about the woodlands,
Soft blue in misty swathe,
The bluebells in their thousands
In dappled sunlight bathe.

Down now in Norton Hollow
The gorse is coming out;
And wheeling swift and swallow
Are always thereabout.

O lovely is the Maytime,
When blackcaps do arrive;
And singing all the daytime
Sound glad to be alive.

Full clear's the springtime weather
And green is all the land,
And youth and love together
Go walking hand in hand.

The hedge was all in white when
The one I love was born;
When softly swayed the aspen
And cuckoos called at dawn.

But May brings down its curtain,
With broom and primrose gone;
Yet this I know for certain,
That Spring in her lives on.

Her smile's of meadow flowers,
Her eyes an azure sky;
And when her voice she lowers
I hear a willow sigh.

In winter's fading twilight
I look up from my chair,
And in her face by firelight,
See apple blossom there.

The Church's New Foundation

The dear old Church of England is getting up-to-date,
By taking on some new ideas, before it is too late.
And Doctor Rowan Williams, Archbishop debonair,
A credit to his Oxfam shop, is leading us with flair.

We've had to make some changes, of that we had no choice;
You've got to keep in step with those who have the loudest voice.
We've weeded out the Old Guard with their Book of Common Prayer,
And with their Rock of Ages, they've gone to sing elsewhere.

We've brought the Hymn-book up-to-date with songs alive and new.
With clapping hands to the tambourines we keep time in the pew.
We learnt the tunes in Tesco's from the jingles playing there,
Promoting cheese and cornflakes, and shampoo for the hair.

Our prayers are nice and chatty now; no more 'Thou' and 'Thee';
Today we talk to God as if He's just like you and me.
He's our management consultant, and when we kneel and pray,
He answers from the great blue sky 'I hear what you say.'

Halfway through the service we turn to left and right,
And greet our nearest neighbour; shake hands with all our might.
We do not really know him and we do not care that much,
But we treat him to a beaming smile to show the Christian touch.

We've shifted Sunday worship to suit the omnibus
Edition of Eastenders; God did not make a fuss.
He knows our time is busy and he fits in where he can.
He knows that he must take his turn, like any other man.

The Sunday evening lesson we do not care for much.
It's read by some old fogey who's completely out of touch.
He reads the old church Bible; though perhaps it serves enough,
To remind us just how frightful was this antiquated stuff.

We much prefer the modern Book in language that we know;
Where we can read the tricky bits and understanding show.
We're not quite sure who wrote it but they're literary men.
It may be Enid Blyton, or it might be Bill and Ben.

A woman parson soon we'll have; a Ms. with smiling teeth,
Attired in robes all Persil white, with trousers underneath.
She'll counsel us and guide us; then lead us by the hand
With forms filled up in triplicate, unto the Promised Land.

No more we dress in stuffy shirts or suits and dresses smart.
For church its sweaters now and jeans; we like to look the part.
After all, if Jesus went in sandals and a beard,
You could say that this way to dress he sort of pioneered.

Politically Correct are we; it's best that way these days,
Though we're a bit confused about all those with funny ways.
We quite approve of married chaps and others of their kind,
But Gay Rights men and lesbians – we can't make up our mind.

Sometimes in church I am alone when some odd duty calls.
A holy presence then I feel in the ancient silent walls.
But we're busy painting murals, hanging mobiles from a rod;
So I think in time it'll go away, this creepy sense of God.

Thank God there's no more mystery, or answers to be sought;
No need to stretch our senses with intellectual thought.
Theology is out of date. We're sure that God would say
That Happy-Clappy's what we want for Christians of today.

At Christmas

Christmas Eve by the firelight,
The flames round the logs leap high.
I idly gaze and my thoughts turn
To Christmases long gone by.
I see in the flames old faces
Come flitting across the years;
Of loved ones and of laughter,
And burdensome times and tears.
But saddest of all that I see there,
As I gaze in the flames dreamy-eyed,
Is the face of one whose love faded,
And flickered, and finally died.

Justice

The farmer, fraught by constant thefts,
 And damage to his farm,
Acquired a large and powerful dog
 To limit further harm.

One night he woke to hear outside
 A rumpus in the yard.
Another break-in had occurred,
 The dog was standing guard.

The loyal dog performed its task,
 And grappling in the mud,
It stopped the burglar in his tracks,
 And left him bathed in blood.

But when the matter came to court
 - It beggars all belief -
It was the farmer who was charged,
 For damage to the thief.

The unsuspecting dog was seized
 And driven miles away,
To an iron barred and padlocked cage
 At the RSPCA.

The charge came up before the Bench
 Who dealt with the offence.
It was a clear-cut legal case,
 No need for common sense.

The criminal has got his rights;
 He's just like you and me;
Even when engaged in crime,
 And where he shouldn't be.

The magistrate rebuked at length
    All those who wild dogs own;
Pontificated on the law,
    And let his will be known.

The Police and local vet were called
    His judgement for to keep.
They took the poor bewildered dog
    And put the thing to sleep.

The magistrate felt pretty smart,
    And pleased with what he'd done,
When reading of it in the press,
    'A simple case, this one.'

'With me the law is safe,' he thought,
    'As solid as Stonehenge.'
Society had shown fair play;
    And taken its revenge.

Just cautioned by the magistrate,
    And back in his own place,
The burglar read the same report;
    With a smirk upon his face.

The thief, the dog, the magistrate,
    The farmer with his grief –
I know which one I'd put to sleep,
    And it wouldn't be the thief.

The Meeting

About thirty five and in scruffy jeans
   He sat with a soda and gin;
With an anxious look to the pub's front door
   Whenever a person came in.

At last came a hesitant girl on her own;
   About the same age I would guess,
With fresh powdered face and well groomed hair,
   And a tastefully chosen dress.

He rose and they spoke, and then they shook hands,
   And she shyly gazed all about;
While he went to the bar to get her a drink,
   Maybe thinking she was a bit stout.

They sat and talked in a quiet way,
   By the smoke from his cigarette.
But we could not tell as we watched them there,
   What each thought of the one they'd just met.

I went to eat in the Inn's back room,
   And my meal went lingering on;
And when I returned to my fireside chair
   The man and the girl had both gone.

True Love

When you bulged out just here and there
    I loved you with a will.
But now it's nearly everywhere
    How strange I love you still.